The

Lectin

Free

COOKBOOK

Dave Robbins

Table of Contents

INTRODUCTION

Despite being little known, lectin avoidance recipes are not new. Humans have understood for many years that foods can have certain compounds that can produce side effects in the human body and since then several techniques have been implemented to avoid them; Soak grains and legumes, do not eat immature fruits, avoid green potatoes, peel hard vegetables, avoid some plant seeds and ferment certain foods. These techniques or tips can improve digestion, in fact, they have been doing for many years and the harmful effects of some foods have been minimized.

Unlike oriental food, this diet is based on what tastes good, what looks good, what can be more profitable, and what can last longer in the refrigerator. These diets are not limited to what our ancestors ate but in the food culture that is transmitted on television.

The diet foods lectin is based on several basic foods. These usually have large amounts of lectins; wheat, corn, soy, sugar, dairy products, meat, and potatoes. The lectin foods are also highly inflammatory.

At first, according to toxicological studies, the lectin dose can produce the poison. The doses of these recipes leave us with the unprecedented levels of overweight and obesity, metabolic syndrome and autoimmune disorders.

However, there is a solution. In fact, the solution has always been with us but it has not been applied in the right way. It is about returning to the food traditions of past generations and seeing a reduction in many of our chronic health problems, especially those that we only thought was "part of life". Maybe our grandparents or great-grandparents did not know the word "lectina", however, they knew very well how to prepare and enjoy the food while minimizing its harmful effects. Thanks to their traditions and modern science we can establish and improve these diets with reduced lectin.

The objective of this book is to demonstrate how wisdom and ancient traditions have been combined with modern science and in this way to elaborate the most delicious recipes that will allow you to reduce inflammations, lose weight and avoid illnesses.

Understanding Lectines

The most well-known lectin, in fact, rejected by many, is gluten. This has been the scourge of people with celiac disease. From crumbs of wheat, barley or rye can be enough to damage the lining of the small intestine and cause malnutrition and other diseases. However, studies and research have shown that it also affects people who do not have celiac disease. These people suffer from the same symptoms and are famous for cumbersome, "non-celiac gluten sensitivity".

However, in the early 1900s, scientists did not even consider gluten as a possible culprit in celiac disease. They had observed it for centuries and documented its effects in medical journals, but its etiology was barely understood. Popular treatments ranged from the odd-1 quart of mussels per day-to almost impossible-200 bananas per week. And yet, nobody thought to point the finger at gluten.

The discovery of gluten as the culprit of celiac disease was not made until a few years ago. Scientists and researchers have been observing and studying since before 1900 when he had not been convicted of causing this disease yet. However, the documentation and publications in medical journals were the ones that helped modern scientists understand their etiology. The common treatments have varied from the strange-1 quart of mussels per day-to almost impossible-200 bananas per week. But nobody imagined that the culprit was gluten.

By the 1940s, a doctor in the Netherlands observed that the death rate of children with celiac disease declined greatly from more than 35% to practically zero during the popular Dutch famine when there was no wheat flour anywhere from the country. After the famine was over and wheat flour was available everywhere, the children went back to eating bread and with this, the mortality rate also increased to its former levels.

But in 1950 scientists were able to establish a strong link between wheat gluten and celiac disease and concluded that this was what caused so much physical damage to the small intestine.

As we can see, there is little knowledge about the lectins. In fact, the known and certified of this compound come from the year 1940. Thanks to these few but effective studies, other modern doctors have made observations as Dr. Steven Gundry did in his clinic and in his book The Plant Paradox. However, the actual mechanism by which lectins cause some people to become ill and overweight is little known and is poorly documented in the scientific literature, with few credible clinical studies in humans on the effects of lectins.[1]

In spite of everything, the effects of a diet low in lectin can be seen in our own bodies comparing them with others who have adopted this type of diet. We could continue waiting for other years so that the research is more accurate and effective so that it can support the protocol, or we could simply remove all those foods that cause us illness or make us feel sick. Next, in this book, we will help you do just that, but first, let's know what science defines lectins.

What Are Lectins?

Lectins are proteins that are attached to carbohydrates. Most living beings (plants, animals, bacteria, and fungi) have this protein and can generate multiple functions and reactions within these organisms. In animals, you can see how it acts by causing cell adhesion, cellular reception, and immunity. In plants, it influences the growth of this and creates a defense against predators.

These proteins only occupy 30% of the food and are concentrated in the skin or shell and in the seeds, in the case of plants. In animals, they are also found when they have maintained or consumed at some point a diet high in lectin (foods with grains and soy).

For human diets, most of the concentrations of this protein are found in grains, legumes, cereals, dairy products and solanaceous plants; tomatoes, potatoes, aubergines, and peppers. Therefore, the recipes found in this book are totally free of these foods.

Even some fruits and vegetables may contain low levels of lectins and can be problematic for some people. Some of these foods are summer and winter squashes, cucumbers and melons. We have implemented these ingredients in some recipes in a moderate way because most people can tolerate them.

What Is Wrong With The Lectins?

What happens with the lectins is that they can damage the superficial layer of the small intestine, allowing small particles of food to flow into the bloodstream, where they provoke an immune response. This process is known as a leaky gut syndrome and may contribute to autoimmune disorders.

In 2015, the journal Alternative Therapies in Health and Medicine published an article explaining that lectins consumed in excess can cause nutrient deficiencies, interrupt digestion and cause severe intestinal damage, all thanks to the ability to hold together a large number of carbohydrates. Venezuelan researchers made another publication where they explained their research a little and observed the disturbing effects of the intestine, the damage to the luminal membranes of the intestine and the interference with the digestion and absorption of nutrients, stimulate changes in the bacterial flora and modulate the state immune of the digestive tract.

To understand it better, lectins damage the cells lining the intestines, causing openings between these cells and preventing the absorption of certain nutrients. Foods that contain these proteins also contain protease inhibitors, which prevent enzymes from breaking down proteins.

However, lectins do not affect everyone in the same way, which is why many people can maintain a diet with basic foods mentioned above. To explain this reality there are several theories. One is that people with dysfunctional enzymes are more susceptible to the lectins that the food possesses. Another theory is that lectins only affect those that already have a permeable membrane in the intestine that could be caused by other factors. Finally, as mentioned before, traditional preparation techniques and methods in global cultures minimize damage to lectins in the human body.

What Not To Eat

There is a large list of foods that have a large number of lectins, this includes all cereals, legumes, dairy products, and solanaceous vegetables. It also includes some seeds and seed oils.

Maybe I can find some food "that should not be eaten" in any of the traditional preparation methods. However, in this book, we will offer recipes that do not contain these ingredients.

If you still want to eat foods that are on the "do not eat" list, here are some tips to prepare and reduce as much lectin as possible:

- Remove the husks and seeds to fruits and vegetables.
- Choose refined grains; white rice, also known as "safe starch".
- When you want to cook legumes, soak in water without salt the night before. Rinse and drain well. Cook in fresh water without salt at a high temperature (212ºF) for at least one hour. Ideally, prepare it in a pressure cooker, but it is not mandatory. A slow cooker does not heat enough to destroy lectins.

Grains

- Barley
- Buckwheat
- Corn
- Oats
- Rice
- Rye
- Wheat

Vegetables

- Beans
- Chickpeas
- Lentils
- Peanuts
- Soy *

* Fermented soy products, such as gluten-free soy sauce, are acceptable in small quantities because the fermentation process destroys most harmful lectins.

Vegetables and Fruits
- Peppers
- Chilies
- Eggplant
- Green beans
- Peas
- Potatoes
- Tomatoes

Dairy Products
- Cheese
- Frozen
- Milk
- Yogurt

Seeds
- Chia
- Pumpkin
- Quinoa
- Sunflower

Oils
- Canola oil
- Corn oil
- Soy oil
- Sunflower oil

What to Eat

To make matters worse, the list of foods that can be eaten is endless!

Fruit

Most fruits are acceptable in these diets, including avocado and coconut, with all its derivatives (coconut flour, coconut milk, coconut water, etc.). However, there are some exceptions such as peppers, tomatoes and aubergines, which are considered botanically as fruits.

Vegetables

All vegetables except those mentioned above are acceptable.

Nuts

As for the nuts, it will depend on the tolerance each person has towards them. But all are acceptable in these recipes, in limited quantities. To avoid severe damage and improve the digestion of nuts, dip them in fresh water for at least 8 hours, rinse and drain well. You can dry them in a dehydrator or simply use them in a recipe. Walnut flours are also acceptable, as well as the products made with them.

Fish

All fish and shellfish are acceptable. Choose wild caught fish sustainably whenever possible. Avoid farm fish, these are fed with grains and soybeans, so they are not a good option.

Poultry and Eggs

All poultry types and eggs are accepted: chicken, turkey, duck, quail, etc. Choose poultry and organic eggs, raised in pastures whenever possible to avoid lectins in grain-fed animals.

Meat

All meat types: veal, pork, lamb, etc. They are acceptable. Choose organic meat, raised in grasses or wild whenever possible to avoid lectins in animals fed with grains.

Fat

- Avocado oil
- Coconut oil
- Olive oil
- Sesame oil
- Butter
- Duck fat

Other

- Broth: if you use broth from a purchase in the store, check the label for peppers and tomatoes. Find soup recipes on pages 136 and 137.
- Coffee
- Dark chocolate (70% cocoa or more)
- Soy sauce without gluten or coconut amino acids
- Herbs
- Olives
- Pepper
- Salt
- Spices: all except chili, paprika, cayenne and those made from Solanaceous plants
- Vinegar, everything except malt vinegar, which contains barley
- Wine

Breakfasts

ROASTED VEGETABLES WITH FRIED EGGS

So this is breakfast with a twist. If you're fed up of having the same, boring cereal or toast for breakfast this is a must try. The flavours in this dish taste lovely together first thing in the morning or after your morning workout, to keep you satisfied until lunchtime. It contains all of the protein, complex carbs and healthy fats our bodies need to keep physically and mentally strong and well. It's also great to eat on most diets.

Special dietary requirements:
Nut free
Vegetarian

Prep time- 10 minutes
Cook time- 25 minutes
Serves 4

Ingredients:
- 4 eggs
- 4 sweet potatoes
- 2 zucchini (halved)m
- 1 fennel bulb (cored)
- 1 red onion (halved)
- 1 teaspoon minced fresh thyme
- 3 tablespoons extra virgin olive oil (divided)
- Salt and pepper to season

Method:

1. Preheat your oven to gas mark 5/ 375f/ 190 c or 170 c on a fan assisted oven.
2. Slice the sweet potatoes, Zucchini and red onion into pieces approx ½ inch thick. Slice the fennel into wedges approx ½ inch thick.
3. Place the vegetables together with the fennel and thyme onto a baking tray and then drizzle with 2 tablespoons of olive oil. Lightly toss to coat the contents of the tray. Season with salt and pepper.
4. Roast the vegetables for 25 minutes or until browned. Do not let the vegetables burn otherwise this will char the flavour.
5. Whilst the vegetables are roasting, bring a skillet pan over a medium heat until piping hot. Add 1 tablespoon of olive oil carefully ensuring the oil does not spit back at you.
6. Heat the oil for 15 seconds before adding the eggs. Fry the eggs for 4-5 minutes ensuring the whites are solid but the yolk is still runny- AKA the perfect runny egg!
7. Serve with the fried eggs topping the vegetables and watch your family smile as they eat.

Nutritional content
341 calories, 16g fat, 10g protein, 42g carbohydrates, 8g fibre

BREAKFAST SAUSAGES WITH APPLE AND SAGE

The perfect lectin free sausage- it tastes so much better than your average sausage and comes with the added benefit of being much healthier and doesn't include lectin.

Special dietary requirements:
Egg free
Nut free
Allergen free

Prep time- 5 minutes
Cook time- 10 minutes
Serves 4

Ingredients:
- 1 pound/ 454g ground pork
- 1 shallot (minced)
- ½ cup peeled apples (minced)
- 1 tablespoon of fresh sage (minced)
- ½ teaspoon salt
- ¼ teaspoon pepper

Method:
1. Place all of the ingredients into a mixing bowl and combine.
2. Over a medium heat on the job, heat a skillet pan until piping hot.
3. **EITHER**

   Crumble the mixture and sauté in the pan until browned- approx 10 minutes

   OR

   Use the mixture to shape and create 8 patties. Place them on the skillet and cook for 5 minutes on each side, until browned.

Nutritional content
341 calories, 29g protein, 24g fat, 3G carbohydrates, <1g fibre

EASY PEASY SWEET POTATO HASH BROWNS

Because no one likes to be boring! Add some flavour to your usual breakfast.

Special dietary requirements:
Egg free
Nut free

Allergen free
Vegan

Prep time: 10 minutes
Cook time: 20 minutes
Serves 4

Ingredients:
4 peeled sweet potatoes
2 tablespoons coconut oil
Sea salt to season

Method:
1. Grate the sweet potatoes and squeezed sour any excess moisture.
2. Using a skillet pan, heat the coconut oil.
3. Place the sweet potatoes into the pan and season with a sprinkle of salt.
4. Avoid stirring as much as possible to let the potatoes crisp up on the outside. Fry for approximately 10 minutes. Flip over and fry for another 10 minutes.

   Nutritional content
   198 calories, 7g fat, 2g protein, 32g carbohydrates, 4g fibre

CREPES WITH STRAWBERRIES

A delightful start to your day, bringing the freshness of the crepes together with the sweetness of the strawberries together for a healthy sweet treat.

Dietary requirements:
Vegetarian

Prep time- 10 minutes

Cook time- 45 minutes

Serves 4

Ingredients:

4 eggs

8 teaspoons coconut oil (divided)

2 cups of strawberries

1 cup of sweet vanilla macadamia mousse

½ cup of unsweetened almond milk

1 tablespoon tapioca starch

1 teaspoon vanilla extract

¼ teaspoon sea salt

2 tablespoons of coconut flour

Method:

1. Preheat oven to 375f/ gas mark 5/ 190 of 170 on fan assisted oven. Coat a baking tray with 1 teaspoon of coconut oil.
2. Place eggs, vanilla and almond milk in a blender to combine. Pulse twice before adding the coconut flour, tapioca starch and salt. Blend the mixture until completely smooth and leave to thicken for 10 minutes.
3. Heat the skillet pan and melt a teaspoon of coconut oil. Next, pour in the thickened mixture and spread to cover the base of the pan. Cook for 1-2 minutes until set. Flip and cook for another 30 secondhand immediately transfer to a plate.
4. Repeat with the remaining mixture, adding more coconut oil as necessary to create beautiful crepes.
5. Fill each crepe with 2 tablespoons of the mousse before folding into burritos.
6. Assemble the burritos on a baking tray and drizzle with 2 teaspoons of coconut oil. Bake in the oven for 20 minutes.
7. Serve the browned crepes with fresh strawberries. This is a firm family favourite.

Nutritional content:

511 calories, 12g protein, 26g carbohydrates, 10g fibre

CHOCOLATE CREPES WITH RASPBERRIES

As above but add ¼ cup of cocoa powder and ¼ cup of almond milk to the mixture. Substitute the strawberries for raspberries and fold ¼ cup of caco nibs to the mousse.

Nutritional content:
511 calories,45g fat, 12g protein, 26g carbs, 10g fibre

SPICE OF CINNAMON GRANOLA

This crunchy granola makes the perfectly healthy breakfast, filling you until lunchtime and the added cinnamon makes your taste buds explode in the morning!

Dietary requirements:
Vegetarian

Prep time- 5 minutes
Cook time- 19 minutes
Serves- 7

Ingredients:
1 egg white
1 teaspoon ground cinnamon
¼ teaspoon ground ginger
2 cups of almonds
2 cups pecans
2 cups of walnuts
¼ teaspoon nutmeg
½ cup coconut oil
1 tablespoon vanilla extract
½ cup brown sugar

½ teaspoon of salt
1 cup of raisins

Method:

1. Preheat the oven to 325f/ gas mark 3/ 170 o or 150 o in a fan assisted oven.
2. Place the nuts in a food processor and mix until coarsest ground.
3. Blend the egg whites and the spices with the coconut oil, brown sugar, vanilla and salt.
4. Pour the blended mixture into the food processor nut mixture and pulse an few times.
5. Pour the mixture onto a baking tray and flatten with a spoon.
6. Bake for 5-7 minutes then stir. Continue to bake for a further 5-7 minutes and stir again. Bake for the last 5 minutes until brown.
7. Allow to cool completely before stirring in the raisins. Store in airtight containers until needed.

Nutritional content:
497 calories, 46g fat, 10g protein, 25g carbohydrates, 7g fibre

CHOCOLATE CRUNCH GRANOLA

Recipe as above then add ¼ cup of unsweetened cocoa powder and ¼ teaspoon salt to the granola. Instead of the raisins, add cocoa nibs.

Nutritional content:
477 calories, 45g fat, 11g protein, 21g carbohydrates, 7g fibre

SAUSAGE, MUSHROOM AND SPINACH FRITTATA

This is a power meal to keep you strong and healthy, frittata similar to an omelette, is perfectly filling to eat for any meal.

Dietary requirements:
Nut free

Prep time- 10 minutes
Cook time- 25 minutes
Serves 4

Ingredients:
8 ounces of crumbled pork sausages
1 cup mushrooms
8 eggs
1 cup chopped spinach
1 shallot (thinly sliced)
1 teaspoon olive oil
Salt and pepper

Method:
1. Preheat the oven to 375f/ gas mark 5/ 190 o or 170 o on a fan assisted oven.
2. Heat a skillet pan over a medium heat on the job. Fry the sausage for approx 5 minutes until browned and then transfer to a dish.
3. Add olive oil to the pan. Once hot, fry the mushrooms and then add the shallot and spinach and fry for 1 minute.
4. Return the sausage to the pan with its juices for added flavour and season with salt and pepper.
5. Add the eggs and cook for 5 minutes. Transfer to the oven and for 5-7 minutes until set.

Nutritional content:

390 calories, 30g fat, 26g protein, 2g carbohydrates, <1g fibre

BACON AND AVOCADO FRITTATA

As above except swap the sausage for 4 slices of applewood smoked bacon for extra flavour. Cook for 10 minutes. Omit the shallot, mushrooms and spinach.
Pour in the eggs and then add slices of avocado in the middle of the pan. Cook for 5 minutes on the stove. Transfer to the oven and cook for a further 5-7 minutes.

Nutritional content:
256 calories, 20g fat, 15g protein, 5g carbs, 3G fibre

VEGETARIAN SWEET POTATO FRITTATA

As above but swap the sausage for sweet potatoes and add the mushroom and spinach. This a really colourful and flavourful vegetarian alternative.
Nutritional content: 258 calories, 14g fat, 14g protein, 17g carbs, 7g fibre

LECTIN FREE COFFEE CAKE

Perfect for afternoon tea as well as any other time of day- because cake makes us happy and even more so when it contains less sugar!

Dietary requirements:
Gluten free
Dairy free
Vegetarian

Prep time- 10 minutes
Cook time- 30 minutes
Serves 12

Ingredients:
3 eggs
2 tablespoons coconut flour
1 cup of brown sugar
½ cup of palm shortening
1 tablespoon vanilla extract
2 cups of blanched almond flour
2 tablespoons ground cinnamon
1 teaspoon salt
1 teaspoon baking soda

For the topping:
¼ cup palm shortening
¼ cup almond flour
1 tablespoon ground cinnamon
¼ cup of brown sugar
¼ teaspoon salt

Method
1. Preheat the oven to 350f/ gas mark 4/ 180 o or 160 on a fan assisted oven. Line a baking dish with parchment paper.
2. Mix the brown sugar and shortening together and beat until thick and creamy.
3. Add eggs and vanilla and whisk.
4. Sift in almond flour, cinnamon, baking soda, coconut flour and salt. Mix and then spread onto the baking sheet.
   For the topping:
   Combine the shortening, almond flour, cinnamon, brown sugar and salt. Mix them all together and spread over the top of the cake mixture.
   Bake for 30 minutes and allow to cool before serving.

Nutritional content

310 calories, 25g fat, 6g protein, 26g carbohydrates, 3g fibre

SAUSAGES AND SWEET POTATO STRATA

Savory pork sausage, thinly sliced sweet potatoes, and fresh thyme baked in a coconut milk and egg custard. This breakfast dish is great for preparing the night before leaving no fussing around only needing to bake it in the morning.

Nutritional content:

Nut free

Prep time: 10 minutes *Cook time:* 55 minutes

Serves: 8

Ingredients:

3 sweet potatoes, thinly sliced to about ⅛-inch thick

1 tablespoon coconut oil

16 ounces Apple Sage Breakfast Sausage 1 cup coconut milk

8 eggs, whisked

1 teaspoon sea salt

½ teaspoon freshly ground
pepper 1 tablespoon
minced fresh thyme

1. Preheat the oven to 375°F/ gas mark 5/ 190c or 170c in a fan assisted oven. Brush the baking dish with the coconut oil.

2. Heat a large skillet and fry the sausage until gently browned and cooked through, approx 5 minutes.

3. In a separate bowl, whisk the coconut milk, eggs, salt, pepper, and thyme.

4. Spread the sweet potato slices into the baking dish, allowing them to overlap slightly. Top with about ⅓ of the sausage. Pour ¼ of the coconut-egg mixture over the sausage.

5. Repeat this process, finishing with the remaining coconut milk. Cover the pan with foil and bake for 40 minutes. Remove the foil and cook for another 10 minutes, until gently browned and bubbling.

Nutritional content

363 calories, 24g fat, 22g protein, 14g carbohydrates, 2g fibre

WINTER VEGETABLES STRATA

Great breakfast or dinner, this seasonal special is lovely comfort food on a winter's day.

Dietary requirements:
Nut free
Vegetarian

Prep time- 5 minutes
Cook time- 45-50 minutes

Serves 4

Ingredients

2 parsnips (cut into 1-inch pieces)

1 sweet potato (cut into 1-
inch pieces)

1 turnip (cut into 1-inch
pieces)

1 fennel bulb (trimmed and cut into 1-inch pieces)

1 red onion (cut into 1-inch pieces)

2 tablespoons minced fresh herbs

8 tablespoons extra-virgin olive oil

8 eggs (whisked)

sea salt, to taste

freshly ground pepper, to taste

Method

1. Preheat the oven to 400f/ gas mark 6/ 200 c or 180 c in a fan assisted oven.
2. In a baking dish, assemble the parsnips, sweet potato, turnip, fennel, onions and herbs. Drizzle with olive oil and season with salt and pepper.
3. Bake for 35 minutes until the vegetables and brown and soft.
4. Season the eggs with salt and add to the baking dish. Bake for 5-10 minutes or until eggs are set. Allow to cool for 5 minutes.

Nutritional content
259 calories, 13g fat, 15g protein, 21g carbohydrates, 5g fibre

BACON, EGG AND BROCCOLI MUFFINS

Great for batch cooking- store in an airtight container and then they make a really easy breakfast when pushed for time.

Dietary requirements
Nut free
Prep time- 10 minutes
Cook time- 15 minutes
Serves 12

Ingredients:
12 eggs
2 cups broccoli
2 green onions
4 slices of bacon (cut into small pieces)
½ teaspoon of salt
¼ teaspoon pepper

1. Preheat the oven to 350f/ gas mark 4/ 180c or 160c if fan assisted oven. Line a 12 cup muffin tray with parchment paper liners.
2. Place equal amounts of the bacon, broccoli and onions in each muffin cup.
3. In a mixing bowl, crack the eggs and add the salt and pepper. Whisk lightly and then pour into the muffin cups.
4. Bake for 15 minutes. Cool and serve.

Nutritional content
93 calories, 6g fat, 7g protein, 1g carbohydrate, 1g fibre

DUTCH BREAKFAST

Lovely and sweet- one for the kids to try served with fresh fruit.

Dietary requirements
Vegetarian
Prep time- 5 minutes
Cook time- 20 minutes
Serves 4

Ingredients
½ cup almond milk
2tablespoons coconut flour
½ cup of tapioca starch
12 Eggs
2   tablespoons maple syrup
2   tablespoons coconut oil
2 tablespoons maple syrup
¼ teaspoon salt
1 tablespoon vanilla extract

Method
1. Preheat the oven to 400f/ gas mark 6/ 200c or 180c in a fan assisted oven.
2. In a blender add the almond milk, eggs, maple syrup, vanilla extract, coconut flour, tapioca starch and salt and blend until the mixture is a smooth purée.
3. Heat the coconut oil in a skillet pan and then add the eggs. Transfer to the oven and bake for 20 minutes until golden and puffy. Serve with a drizzle of maple syrup.

Nutritional content
326 calories, 22g fat, 20g protein, 12g carbohydrates, 2g fibre
Snacks

ASIAN STYLE CHICKEN WINGS

These are great on their own or served with a green salad. This recipe omits the nightshades found in most other recipes. Marinade chicken overnight before cooking for best results.

Dietary requirements
Egg free
Nut free
Prep time- 5 minutes
Cook time- 30 minutes
Serves 6

Ingredients
　　1 pound of chicken wings
　　2 gloves garlic
　　1 lime
　　2 tablespoons toasted sesame oil
　　¼ cup gluten free soy sauce
　　½ teaspoon pepper
　　2 tablespoons minced ginger

Method
1. Preheat the oven to 425f/ gas mark 7, 220c or 200c in a fan assisted oven. Line a baking sheet with parchment paper.
2. Add garlic, lime (juice and zest), soy sauce, sesame oil, ginger and pepper to a blender and purée until smooth to produce a marinade.
3. Put the chicken wings in a bowl and then fully coat each wing with the marinade.
4. Assemble the chicken wings onto the baking tray and cook in the oven for 30 minutes.

Nutritional content
276 calories, 8g fat, 38g protein, 2g carbohydrates, 0g fibre

AVOCADO ON SWEET POTATO TOAST

Be bang on trend and avoid this pesky grains by substituting bread for sweet potato toast.

Dietary requirements
Egg free
Nut free
Allergen free
Vegan

Ingredients
2 Sweet potatoes (sliced)
2 Avocados (thinly sliced)
1 tablespoon canola oil/ coconut oil
1 teaspoon red wine vinegar
Salt and pepper

Method
1. Preheat he oven to 375f/ gas mark 5/ 190c or 170c in a fan assisted oven. Line a baking sheet with parchment paper.
2. In a bowl, cover the potatoes with the oil and then place on the baking tray and season with salt.
3. Bake for 30 minutes until caramelized and shrunken. Cook for 5 minutes.
4. Serve with Avocado topping the sweet potato slices. Season with salt and pepper and add a splash of red wine vinegar.

Nutritional content 243 calories, 17g fat, 3g protein, 23g carbohydrates, 8g fibre

SMOKED SALMON AND AVOCADO ON SWEET POTATO TOAST

A mixture of salty and creamy textures to awaken the senses and a fantastic alternative to smoked salmon and cream cheese bagels.

Dietary requirements
Egg free
Nut free
Prep time- 5 minutes
Cook time- 30 minutes
Serves 4

Ingredients
2 sliced sweet potatoes
½ cup sliced red onion
1 tablespoon canola/ coconut oil
2 Avocados (thinly sliced)
2 tablespoons capers
2 tablespoons red wine vinegar
4 ounces smoked salmon
Salt and pepper

Method
1. Preheat the oven to 375f/ gas mark 5/ 190c or 170 c in a fan assisted oven. Line a baking sheet with parchment paper.
2. Coat the potatoes in oil and then place on the baking sheet and season with salt.
3. Bake for 30 minutes and then allow to cool for 5 minutes.
4. Whilst they are cooking, mix onion, salt and vinegar in a bowl and leave to rest. Once the potatoes have cooked, remove the onions from the vinegar.
5. To serve- assemble the slices of sweet potatoes on a plate and top with avocado, slice of smoked salmon, red onion and capers. Season with salt and pepper.

Nutritional content
285 calories, 18g fat, 8g protein, 25g carbohydrates, 8g fibre

ZA'ATAR AVOCADO ON SWEET POTATO TOAST

Using spices from the Middle East gives this dish a twist.

Dietary requirements
Egg free
Nut free
Allergen free
Vegan
Prep time- 5 minutes
Cook time- 30 minutes
Serves 4

Ingredients
2 Sweet Potatoes
1 tablespoon canola or coconut oil
1 tablespoon Za'atar
1 tablespoon tahini
1 tablespoon lemon juice
1 tablespoon extra virgin oil
½ cup sliced red onion
Salt

Method
1. Preheat the oven to 375f/ gas mark 5/ 190c or 170c in a fan assisted oven. Line a baking sheet with parchment paper.
2. Coat the potatoes in the oil and then place on the baking sheet and season with salt. Bake for 30 minutes. Allow to cool for 5 minutes.

3. In a bowl, whisk the lemon juice, olive oil and tahini to make the dressing.
4. To serve- top the potato slices with avocado and red onions. Drizzle the dressing over the creation and then finish with a pinch of Za'atar.

Nutritional content
243 calories, 17g fat, 3g protein, 23g carbohydrates, 8g fibre

BACON AND AVOCADO ON SWEET POTATO TOAST

These are great when your craving crisps/ potato chips. They are also perfect party food and canapés.

Dietary requirements
Egg free
Nut free
Allergen free
Prep time- 5 minutes
Cook time- 30 minutes
Serves 4

Ingredients
2Sweet Potatoes
2Avocados
1tablespoon canola/ coconut oil
4slices of bacon
2tablespoons minced fresh chives
Salt and pepper

Method
1. Preheat the oven to 375f/ gas mark 5/ 190c or 170c in a fan assisted oven. Line a baking sheet with parchment paper.

2. Coat the potatoes in the oil and then place on the baking sheet and season with salt.
3. Bake for 30 minutes and then allow to cool for 5 minutes.
4. To serve- top each potato slice with Avocado, bacon and chives. Season with salt and pepper.

Nutritional content
287 calories, 29g fat, 6g protein, 23g carbohydrates, 8g fibre

ROOT VEG BAKED CRISPS/ POTATO CHIPS

These are so healthy and a great alternative to usual potato chips/ crisps.

Dietary requirements
Egg free
Nut free
Allergen free
Vegan
Prep time- 5 minutes
Cook time- 15 minutes
Serves 4

Ingredients
1 pound of assorted root vegetables (beets, sweet potatoes, turnips) sliced paper thin
2 tablespoons canola or coconut oil
Salt

Method
1. *Preheat the oven to 350f/ gas mark 4/ 180c or 160c in a fan assisted oven.*
2. *Coat veg slices in the oil and assemble on a baking sheet without overlapping. Season with salt.*

3. *Bake for 15 minutes until crisp and browning. Allow to cool and then season with salt.*

Nutritional content
157 calories, 7g fat, 2g protein, 23g carbohydrates, 3g fibre

GRILLED MUSHROOM SKEWERS

These can be served as a snack or as an accompaniment to a main meal.

Dietary requirements
Egg free
Nut free
Allergen free
Vegan

Prep time- 5 minutes
Cook time- 5 minutes
Serves 4

Ingredients
1 pint of Cremini mushrooms
1 shallot (chopped)
2 tablespoons fresh thyme
¼ cup roughly chopped cilantro
2 cloves garlic (minced)
¼ cup extra virgin olive oil
2 tablespoons sherry vinegar
Salt and pepper

Method

1. Add thyme, shallot, cilantro, garlic, sherry vinegar, olive oil and salt and pepper to a blender and mix into a smooth purée to make a marinade.
2. Thread the mushrooms through skewers and coat in the marinade.
3. Grill for 5 minutes and serve immediately.

Nutritional content

142 calories, 14g fat, 1g protein, 4g carbohydrates, 1g fibre

Soups, Salads and Sides

FRESH HERB SALAD WITH GINGER LIME VINAIGRETTE

This zesty salad is perfect for summer months and a great accompaniment with your main of fish or meat. Fast and easy- there's no excuse not to try this one.

Dietary requirements
Egg free
Nut free
Allergen free
Vegetarian
Prep time- 5 minutes
Cook time- n/a
Serves 4

Ingredients
2 cups mixed herbs eg mint, cilantro, basil
1 teaspoon minced ginger
1teaspoon honey
2tablespoons lime juice
2tablespoons extra virgin olive oil
4cups mixed salad greens included spinach
salt and pepper

Method
1. In a bowl add the honey, ginger, lime juice and olive oil and whisk together to create a dressing. Season with salt and pepper.

2. Add the green salad and the herbs and toss to coat in the dressing. Serve to your family with fresh cold drinks.

Nutritional content
81 calories, 7g fat, 1g protein, 1g carbohydrates, 2g fibre

ROMAINE HEARTS WITH DIJON AND SCALLION DRESSING

Great as a side dish with steak.

Dietary requirements
Egg free
Nut free
Allergen free
Vegan
Prep time- 5 minutes
Cook time- none
Serves 4

Ingredients
4green parts of scallions (diced)
2Romaine hearts (chopped)
2tablespoons white wine vinegar
½ bunch parsley
1 tablespoon Dijon mustard
1 lemon (zest and juice)
¼ cup extra virgin olive oil
Salt

Method
1. Wash the romaine lettuce to clean and place in a large bowl once chopped.

2. To make the dressing add the rest of the ingredients to a blender and create a smooth purée. Serve over the lettuce.

Nutritional content
135 calories, 14g fat, 2g protein, 3g carbohydrates, 2g fibre

KALE AND GREEN GODDESS SALAD

Fresh tarragon gives this dish it's signature flavour. The dressing used mayo to keep the recipe low lectin.

Prep time- 5 minutes
Cook time- none
Serves 4

Ingredients
1head of kale (washed and chopped)
2tablespoons minced tarragon
2tablespoons minced chives
¼ cup minced parsley
1teaspoon minced garlic
1tablespoon lemon juice
1 teaspoon anchovy paste
¼ cup chopped pistachios
Salt

Method
1. In a large bowl, add the chopped kale and olive oil. Coat the kale.
2. To make the dressing place the garlic, tarragon, parsley, chives, lemon juice, anchovy paste and mayo in a blender to create a smooth purée. Drizzle the dressing over the top of the kale and top with some pistachios.

Nutritional content
218 calories, 16g fat, 7g protein, 17g carbohydrates, 6g fat

CLASSIC FRENCH ONION SOUP

This beautiful dish is naturally nightshade free although check the label on the beef broth as some contain added ingredients.

Dietary requirements
Egg free
Nut free
Allergen free

Prep time- 10 minutes
Cook time- 80 minutes
Serves 4

Ingredients
3onions (thinly sliced)
¼ cup dry red wine
1quart beef broth
2tablespoons olive oil
1sprig thyme
1 sprig rosemary
Salt

Method
1. In a large pan on the hob, cook the onions with a dash of salt in olive oil for 30 minutes with the lid on.
2. Take the lid off for the last 30 minutes and cook until golden brown.

3. Add thyme, rosemary, broth and red wine and simmer for 20 minutes. Remove the herbs before serving.

Nutritional content
125 calories, 6g fat, 7g protein, 9g carbohydrates, 2g fat.

CHICKEN AND FRENCH ONION SOUP

This soup is amazing if you add pieces of chicken thighs just before adding the red wine and broth. Brown the chicken and then add the broth, red wine and herbs. Simmer until the chicken is cooked.

Nutritional content
273 calories, 11g fat, 32g protein, 9g carbohydrates, 2g fibre

PARSNIP SOUP WITH BALSAMIC RED ONIONS

Dietary requirements
Egg free
Nut free
Allergen free
Vegan
Prep time- 10 minutes
Cook time-30 minutes
Serves 4

Ingredients
1 pound parsnips
1 onion (sliced)
1 red onion (thinly sliced)

1 tablespoon balsamic vinegar

1 tablespoon maple syrup

1 cup coconut milk

1 ½ tablespoons extra virgin olive oil

½ teaspoon minced garlic

¾ teaspoon sea salt

½ teaspoon pepper

1½ teaspoon minced rosemary

4cups veg broth

Method

1. On the hob heat a large pan heat 1 tablespoon olive oil. Add the yellow onion and cook on a medium heat until soft but not browned approx 8 minutes. Add garlic and fry for 1 minute.
2. Add parsnips, broth, coconut milk and salt. Add a lid to the pan and simmer for 20 minutes.
3. While the soup is cooking heat ½ tablespoon oil in a skillet pan.
4. Add the red onion, pepper, rosemary and ¼ teaspoon salt. Fry for 2 minutes before reducing the heat and then cook until the onions caramelise. Add the balsamic vinegar and maple syrup.
5. Purée the soup in a blender and serve with the onions topping the soup.

Nutritional content
288 calories, 17g fat, 4g protein, 34g carbohydrates, 6g fibre

SPINACH AND SWEET POTATO SOUP

You can add 1 teaspoon of paprika if you don't have an issue with nightshades.

Dietary requirements

Egg free

Nut free

Allergen free
Prep time- 10 minutes
Cook time- 30 minutes
Serves 4

Ingredients
4Sweet Potatoes (diced)
4cups chopped spinach
2spring onions (thinly sliced)
1 quart chicken OR Veg broth
1 diced onion
1 tablespoon minced garlic
1 tablespoon ground cumin
1 can coconut milk
1 tablespoon coconut oil
Sea salt

Method
1. Heat the coconut oil on the hob in a large pan.
2. Fry the onions for 9 minutes until golden brown and soft.
3. Stir in the garlic and cumin and fry for 1 minute.
4. Add the sweet potatoes, broth, salt and pepper and simmer in a covered pan for 15 minutes.
5. Stir in the coconut milk and after a minute add the spinach and spring onions and cook for 1 minute. Serve immediately.
6.

Nutritional content
373 calories, 23g fat, 5g protein, 40g carbohydrates, 5g fibre

COCONUT CELERIAC PURÉE

This makes a creamy side dish and an awesome potato substitute.

Dietary requirements
Egg free
Nut free
Allergen free
Prep time- 5 minutes
Cook time- 30 minutes
Serves 4

Ingredients
1celeriac (peeled and sliced into 1 inch pieces)
2cups of chicken broth
1sprig fresh thyme
1 clove garlic
1 can coconut milk
Salt

Method
1. In a large panels e the celeriac, thyme, garlic, coconut milk, chicken broth, and salt and cover with a lid. Simmer for 30 minutes.
2. Remove the thyme and drain the celeriac leaving the juices aside.
3. Purée the celeriac and 1 cup of the juices. Serve freshly cooked.

Nutritional content
211 calories, 11g fat, 5g protein, 25g carbohydrates, 5g fibre

ROASTED GARLIC CAULIFLOWER

Dietary requirements
Egg free

Prep time- 5 minutes
Cook time- 10 minutes
Serves 4

Ingredients
1 cauliflower broken up into florets
½ cup chicken broth
¼ cup coconut cream
1 tablespoon roasted garlic
½ teaspoon white wine vinegar
½ teaspoon salt

Method
1. Steam the cauliflower for 10 minutes.
2. Place the cauliflower in a food processor with broth, coconut cream, garlic, vinegar and salt. Blend to make a smooth purée. Served while hot.

Nutritional content
92 calories, 6g fat, 3g Protein, 9g carbohydrates, 4g fibre

ROASTED CARROT WITH CARROT LEAVES PESTO

Dietary requirements
Egg free
Nut free
Allergen free
Vegan
Prep time- 10 minutes
Cook time- 25 minutes

Serves 4

Ingredients

1 bunch of carrots with stems

4 tablespoons extra virgin olive oil

1/2 cup basil

1 clove garlic

1 tablespoon minced red onion

2tablespoons lemon juice

Salt and pepper

Method

1. Preheat the oven to 375f/ gas mark 5/ 190c or 170c in a fan assisted oven.
2. Place the carrots on baking tray and pour over 1 tablespoon olive oil to coat. Season with salt. Roast for 25 minutes.
3. While cooking, add to a blender the red onion, lemon juice, basil, garlic and 3 tablespoons olive oil. Chop the stems and add to the blender. Pulse until well combined and then season with salt and pepper.
4. To serve- top the roasted carrots with the pesto.

Nutritional content

165 calories, 14g fat, 1g protein, 11g carbohydrates, 3g fibre

MASHED PLANTAINS WITH BACON

Dietary requirements

Egg free

Nut free

Allergen free

Prep time- 5 minutes

Cook time- 26 minutes
Serves 4

Ingredients
2plantains (slices)
2Slices applewood smoked bacon (sliced)
½ cup fennel (thinly sliced)
Cooking oil (as needed)
1 teaspoon minced garlic
Sea salt

Method
1. Fry the bacon in a large skillet pan for 10 minutes. Put the bacon in a bowl but keep the fat in the pan.
2. Fry the fennel in the bacon fat for 5 minutes add the garlic and fry for 1 minute. Put he garlic and fennel with the bacon in the bowl.
3. Cook the plantains in the same pan (use oil if needed) for 5 minutes each side. Mash them to look like mashed potatoes. Add the fennel and garlic and bacon and mash until mixed together. Season with salt

Nutritional content
199 calories, 5g fat, 5g protein, 37g carbs, 3g fibre

GINGER RAINBOW CHARD

Dietary requirements
Egg free
Nut free
Allergen free
Vegan
Prep time- 5 minutes

Cook time- 5 minutes
Serves 4

Ingredients
1 bunch rainbow chard (diced stems and sliced leaves)
1 teaspoon minced garlic
1 teaspoon sesame oil
1 tablespoon extra virgin olive oil
   1   teaspoon minced ginger
2tablespoons coconut aminos/ gluten free soya sauce
1 teaspoon maple syrup
1 teaspoon lime juice

Method
1. In a skillet pan, heat both the olive oil and the sesame oil and then add the chard, ginger and garlic.
2. Sauté for 3-4 minutes
3. Whisk together the coconut, maple syrup and lime juice and then add to the pan of chard. Cook together for 2 minutes. Serve whilst hot.

Nutritional content
87 calories, 5g fat, 4g protein, 10g carbohydrates, 4g fibre

APPLES AND CRISP SAGE

Dietary requirements
Egg free
Nut free
Allergen free
Vegan
Prep time- 5 minutes

Cook time- 12 minutes

Serve 4

Ingredients

4 apples (peeled and sliced into wedges)

8 Sage leaves

2 tablespoons extra virgin olive oil

1 red onion (thinly sliced)

¼ teaspoon cinnamon

¼ teaspoon minced garlic

1 teaspoons lemon juice

Salt

Method

1. Heat the oil in a skillet pan on the hob. Fry the sage leaves for 5 seconds and then leave on a cooling rack to crisp.
2. Add the apples and onions and cook for 10 minutes.
3. Add the garlic and cinnamon and cook for 2 minutes. Squeeze in the lemon juice and add a pinch of salt. Top with the crisp sage leaves to serve.

Nutritional content

141 calories, 7g fat, 1g protein, 22g carbohydrates, 4g fibre

COCONUT ROASTED SWEET POTATOES

Dietary requirements

Egg free

Nut free

Allergen free

Vegan

Prep time- 5 minutes
Cook time- 30 minutes
Serves 4

Ingredients
4 Sweet Potatoes (cut into pieces)
2 tablespoons melted coconut oil
Sprinkle of salt

Method
1. Preheat the oven to 375f/ gas mark 5/ 190c or 170c in a fan assisted oven.
2. Assemble on a baking sheet and add oil over the potatoes.
3. Bake for 30 minutes

Nutritional content
196 calories, 7g fat, 7g protein, 32g carbohydrates, 4g fibre

SWEET POTATO SALAD WITH PISTACHIOS

Dietary requirements
Egg free
Vegetarian
Prep time- 5 minutes
Cook time- none
Serves 4

Ingredients
Sweet potatoes roasted as above
2tablespoons extra virgin olive oil
¼ cup chopped pistachios
2tablespoons minced shallots

¼ minced parsley

¼ teaspoon salt

1 teaspoon honey

1tablespoons sherry vinegar

Method
1. Place the roasted sweet potatoes on the serving plates.
2. Chop the pistachios and leave to the side.
3. With the remaining ingredients mix together to create a dressing. Pour over the potatoes and then finish by topping with the potatoes.

Nutritional content
300 calories, 17g fat, 4g protein, 34g carbohydrates, 5g fibre

ROASTED GARLIC SPROUTS

When you roast, they produce a lighter flavour. Team these with your main course for a healthy side dish.

Dietary requirements

Egg free

Nut free

Allergen free

Vegetarian

Prep time- 5 minutes

Cook time- 30 minutes

Serves 4

Ingredients

1 pound sprouts (peeled and cut in half)

2tablespoons extra virgin olive oil

1 teaspoon honey

1 teaspoon minced garlic

1 tablespoon red wine vinegar

Salt

Pepper

Method
1. Preheat the oven to 375f/ gas mark 5/ 190c or 170 in a fan assisted oven
2. Place sprouts on a baking sheet and drizzle with oil.
3. Cook in the oven for 30 minutes.
4. Whilst they are cooking, whisk together vinegar honey, garlic and olive oil to make a dressing.
5. To serve top the sprouts with the dressing.

Nutritional content
173 calories, 14g fat, 4g protein, 11g carbohydrates, 5g fibre

BALSAMIC BRUSSEL SPROUTS

As above but add 1 tablespoon of honey and 2 tablespoons balsamic vinaigrette after 25 minutes of cooking instead of red wine vinegar and garlic. Cook for 5 minutes before serving.

Nutritional content
179 calories, 14g fat, 4g protein, 13g carbohydrates, 5g fibre

HOLIDAYS SWEET POTATO DRESSING

This tastes the same as turkey stuffing so perfect diet food over the holidays/ Christmas time.

Dietary requirements
Egg free
Nut free
Allergen free
Prep time- 10
Cooking time- 60 minutes
Serves 6

Ingredients
3sweet potatoes
½ cup chicken broth
3celery sticks
2tablespoons parsley
2tablespoons sage
1tablespoon thyme
1onion (diced)
3tablespoons extra virgin olive oil
Salt
Pepper

Method
1. Preheat the oven to 375f/ gas mark 5/ 190c or 170 in a fan assisted oven.
2. Spread the sweet potatoes across a baking tray and sprinkle over the herbs before adding the oil and some salt and pepper.
3. Roast the potatoes for 35 minutes.
4. After cooking for 25 minutes, fry some celery and onion and then stir the sweet potatoes into the pan.
5. Add the chicken broth and cover with a lid. Let it cook for 15 minutes.
6. Place in a fridge overnight and cook for 25 minutes before serving.

Nutritional content .

153   Calories, 7g fat, 2g protein, 21g carbohydrates, 4g fibre

CAULIFLOWER AND RAISIN ROAST NUT MIX

Winter comfort food- crunchy and wholesome brings the cauliflower alive.

Dietary requirements
Egg free
Vegan
Prep time- 5 minutes
Cook time- 30 minutes
Serves 4

Ingredients
1 cauliflower
¼ cup raisins
1tablespoon minced garlic
¼ cup minced parsley
1teaspoon lemon zest
1 tablespoons extra virgin olive oil
2tablespoons red wine vinegar
¼ cup pine nuts
Salt and pepper

Method
1. Preheat the oven to 375f/ gas mark 5/ 190c or 170 in a fan assisted oven.
2. In a bowl, coat the cauliflower along with the garlic, parsley, lemon zest in the oil.
3. Spread the Cauliflower on a baking tray and roast for 30 minutes.
4. To serve, toss with raisins and red wine vinegar and top with pine nuts

Nutritional content
175 calories, 12g fibre, 4g protein, 17g carbohydrates, 5g fibre

BEETROOTS IN MAPLE SYRUP

Dietary requirements

Egg free

Nut free

Allergen free

Vegan

Prep time- 10 minutes

Cook time- 35 minutes

Serves 4

Ingredients

2bundles of beets

¼ cup maple syrup

¼ cup red wine vinegar

2tablespoons extra virgin olive oil

salt

Pepper

Method
1. Preheat the oven to 375f/ gas mark 5/ 190c or 170c in a fab assisted oven.
2. Cut the beetroot into quarters and place on a baking tray before pouring over come olive oil.
3. Roast for 25 minutes.
4. Whisk maple syrup and red wine together and pour over the roast beetroot. Cook for another 15 minutes to produce a thick glaze.

Nutritional content

145 calories, 7g fat, 1g protein, 21g carbohydrates, 2g fat

FISH AND SEAFOOD

STEAMED CLAMS IN WHITE WINE

Restaurant quality without the unhealthy butter

Prep time- 10 minutes
Cook time- 17 minutes
Serves 4

Ingredients
2lb fresh clams
½ cup dry white wine
1 minced onion
1 tablespoon minced garlic
2cups chicken broth
2tablespoons extra virgin olive oil
2sprigs thyme
¼ cup minced parsley
Juice of ½ lemon
Salt
Pepper

Method
1. Fry onion and garlic in oil in a large pan for 5 minutes until soft.
2. Pour in the white wine and cook for 2 minutes to reduce the alcohol.
3. Add chicken broth, clams, thyme and salt and pepper and then give it a stir.
4. Cover the pan with a lid and leave to simmer for 10 minutes to allow the clams to steam open. Remove the springs of time.
5. Serve with the parsley garnish and squeezed lemon juice.

STEAMED MUSSELS BROTH

Dietary requirements
Egg free
Nut free
Prep time- 10 minutes
Cook time- 17 minutes
Serves 4

Ingredients
2lb fresh mussels
1 Tarragon sprigs
2 cups chicken broth
1 cup coconut milk
1 teaspoon minced garlic
1 teaspoon coconut oil
2 shallots (thinly sliced)
Salt and pepper

Method
1. Fry shallots and garlic in a large pan over the stove until soft approx 5 minutes.
2. Add white wine and cook for 2 minutes.
3. Add coconut milk, tarragon, mussels and chicken broth and stir around. Add salt and pepper.
4. Cover with a lid and allow to simmer for 10 minutes until the mussels open.

Nutritional content
534 calories, 24g fat, 55g protein, 21g carbohydrates, 0g fibre

CRAB CAKES

Prep time- 5 minutes
Cook time- 15 minutes
Serves 4

Ingredients
1lb crab meat
½ cup garlic aioli
1 egg white
¼ cup almond flour
½ cup mayo
2 tablespoons seafood seasoning blend
1 Cloves garlic minced
2 tablespoons coconut oil
1 Scallion minced

Method
1. Whisk the scallion, seasoning blend, garlic, mayo, egg white, both flours and salt and then fold in the crab meat.
2. Make into 6 patties and put in the fridge for at least 1 hour to set.
3. Fry the crab cakes in coconut oil for 5-7 minutes on each side.
4. Finish with a drizzle of garlic aioli

Nutritional content
481 calories, 38g fat, 28g protein, 5g carbohydrates, 2g fibre

HAZELNUT HALIBUT

Egg free
Prep time- 5 minutes
Cook time- 5 minutes
Serves 4

Ingredients
4halibut fillets
½ cup hazelnuts
1 teaspoon garlic powder
½ teaspoon salt
½ teaspoon pepper
1   tablespoons coconut oil

Method
1. Grind the hazel nuts in a spice grinder and leave to the side.
2. In a blender, pulse (twice) garlic and salt and pepper.
3. Coat the Halibut in the hazelnuts before cooking in a pan over the hob for 2-3 minutes
4. Finish by adding the garlic over the halibut.
5.

Nutritional content
402 calories, 22g fat, 48g protein, 3g carbohydrates, 2g fibre

PISTACHIOS CRUSTED HALIBUT

Simply replace the hazelnuts for pistachios and add 2 tablespoons minced parsley.

Nutritional content
382 calories, 19g fat, 49g carbohydrates, 2g fibre

TUNA PROVENÇAL

This is great serves with salad and olives.

Dietary requirements
Egg free
Nut free
Prep time- 5 minutes
Cook time- 15 minutes
Serves 4

Ingredients
2lbs tuna (1/2 thick pieces)
2sprigs rosemary
4sprigs thyme
6cloves garlic
½ red onion (thinly sliced)
Salt and pepper

Method
1. Preheat the oven to 325f/ gas mark 3/ 170c or 150 in a fan assisted oven.
2. Place the tuna across the baking tray and season with salt and pepper and rosemary and thyme. On top of this, sprinkle the onion and garlic and finally olive oil.
3. Cover with foil and bake for 12 minutes. Serve warm.

Nutritional content
302 calories, 10g fat, 50g protein, 8g carbohydrates, 0g fibre

SCALLOPS WITH SPINACH

Dietary requirements
Egg free
Nut free
Prep time- 10 minutes
Cook time- 6 minutes
Serves 2-4

Ingredients
6cups spinach
1teaspoon garlic
1tablespoon extra virgin olive oil
1tablespoon lemon juice
Salt and pepper

Method
1. Season with salt and pepper on both sides of the scallops and then fry for 2 minutes each side. Place on a serving dish.
2. Fry the garlic and spinach for 2 minutes before serving with the scallops and topping with the lemon juice.

Nutritional content
284 calories, 9g fat, 41g protein, 9g carbohydrates, 2g fibre

SCALLOPS WRAPPED IN PROSCIUTTO

Dietary requirements
Egg free
Nut free
Prep time- 10 minutes

Cook time- 6 minutes
Serves 2

Ingredients
1 lb scallops
8 slices prosciutto
1 tablespoon extra virgin olive oil
Salt and pepper

Method
1. Pat dry scallops and wrap a slice of prosciutto around each one. Season
2. Fry the scallops for 2 minutes on each side ensuring the prosciutto stays wrapped around them.
3. Serve immediately

Nutritional content
296 calories, 11g fat, 41g protein, 6g carbohydrates, 0g fibre

ASIAN TUNA IN SESAME SEEDS

Dietary requirements
Egg free
Nut free
Prep time- 5 minutes
Cook time- 6 minutes
Serves 4

Ingredients
4tuna steaks
½ cup sesame seeds
1teaspoon sesame oil

1 tablespoon canola oil
Salt and pepper

Method
1. Season the tuna with salt and pepper on both sides and then coat in sesame seeds.
2. Fry the tuna in sesame seed oil and canola oil for 1 minute on each side (to produce rare)

Nutritional content
324 calories, 169g fat, 41g protein, 10g carbohydrates, 2g fibre

SALMON CAKES

Dietary requirements
Nut free
Prep time- 10 minutes
Cook time- 28 minutes
Serves 4

Ingredients
1 cup diced sweet potatoes
2 egg
2green onions
1 can salmon
1 tablespoons coconut oil
2 tablespoons coconut flour
Salt and pepper

Method
1. Steam sweet potato for 10 minutes.

2. Mash the cooked potatoes in a bowl and then and the onions, coconut flour, egg and salt and pepper and finally stir in the salmon.
3. Make 8 patties with the mixture and keep in the fridge for at least an hour.
4. Fry in the coconut oil for at least 4 minutes on each side.

Nutritional content
289 calories, 16g fat, 25g protein, 11g carbohydrates, 3g fibre

TUNA BURGERS

As above but replace the salmon for tuna. Add ½ cup celery and serve in a bun.

Nutritional content
388 calories, 27g fat, 25g protein, 72g carbohydrates, 3g fibre

CRUSTED SALMON BROCCOLINI

Dietary requirements
Egg free
Prep time- 10 minutes
Cook time- 9 minutes
Serves 4

Ingredients
1 ½ lb salmon
1 bunch broccolini
¼ cup ground pine nuts
2cloves garlic

1cup basil

1teaspoon lemon juice

¼ cup extra virgin olive oil

Salt and pepper

Method

1. In a blender, purée the basil, lemon juice, olive oil and garlic to make a pesto and set aside for later.
2. Sauté the broccoli in oil for 5 minutes and then add garlic for 30 seconds. Transfer to a plate.
3. Season the salmon before costing in the pine nuts.
4. Gently dear the salmon on each side for 2 minutes.
5. To serve, pour the pesto over the salmon.

Nutritional content

484 calories, 33g fat, 39g protein, 10g carbohydrates, 6g fibre

GARLIC SHRIMP FETTUCCINE

Prep time- 10 minutes

Cook time- 5 minutes

Serves 2

Ingredients

12 ounces Shrimp

Grain free Fettuccine

2tablespoons parsley

1tablespoon minced garlic

2tablespoons lemon juice

Salt

Pepper

Method

1. Fry the shrimp on a skillet on the stove for 4 minutes and then add the garlic and cook for 1 minute. Season with salt and pepper and the lemon juice and add to a mixing bowl.
2. Cook the Fettuccine in boiling water for 90 seconds. Drain and add to the bowl of shrimp. Mix together and place on serving plates with parsley to garnish.

Nutritional content
549 calories, 28g fat, 43g protein, 32 carbohydrates, 2g fibre

PESTO AND SHRIMP FETTUCCINE

Instead of garlic and parsley in the previous recipe add 1 cup pesto after adding the cooked Fettuccine.

Nutritional content
714 calories, 44g fat, 46g protein, 37g carbohydrates, 6g fibre

SHRIMP AND BOL CHOY STIR FRY

Prep time- 10 minutes
Cook time- 15 minutes
Serves 4
Egg free

Ingredients
1lb shrimp
12 heads Bok choy

1 cup mushrooms

2 tablespoons coconut oil

1 teaspoon sesame oil

1 tablespoon minced garlic

1 tablespoon minced ginger

4 green onions (sliced)

¼ gluten free soy sauce

½ chicken broth

1j uice lime

1 teaspoon honey

1 tablespoon arrowroot powder

Method
1. Cook the shrimp for 5 minutes in a skillet pan over the stove and then put on a plate.
2. Heat the coconut oil and the sesame oil in the skillet and fry the bok choy for 3 minutes on both sides.
3. Add onions, mushrooms, ginger and garlic to the pan with the bok choy and fry for 2 minutes.
4. In a bowl whisk the chicken broth, soy sauce, lime juice, honey, arrowroot powder and then pour into a pan and cook for 2 minutes.

Nutritional content
219 calories, 9g fat, 27g protein, 7g carbohydrates, 1g fibre

SHRIMP AND GREEN STIR FRY

Instead of Bok Choy and mushrooms use trimmed green beans and a sliced leek. Cook for 8 minutes.

MAHI MAHI WITH PINEAPPLE AND MANGO SALSA

Prep time- 10 minutes
Cook time- 5 minutes
Serves 4
Egg free
Nut free

Ingredients
4 mahi mahi steaks
1 cup diced pineapple
1 diced mango
1 tablespoons lime juice
¼ cup minced red onions
¼ cup minced cilantro
1 minced glove garlic
1 tablespoon coconut oil
Salt and pepper

Method
1. In a bowl, mix together the mango, pineapple, lime juice, garlic, onions and cilantro salt and pepper. Set aside for later.
2.   Coat the mahi mahi in coconut oil and season with salt and pepper.
3. Grill for 5 minutes on each side and serve with the salsa.

Nutritional content
270 calories, 6g fat, 41g protein, 15g carbohydrates, 2g fibre

MAHI MAHI TACOS WITH PINEAPPLE AND MANGO SALSA

As above but serve in grain free tortillas and top each one with cabbage strips and garlic aioli.

Nutritional content
511 calories, 25g fat, 41g protein, 40g carbohydrates, 5g fibre

SMOKED SALMON CASSEROLE

Prep time- 15 minutes
Cook time- 60 minutes
Serves 4
Nut free

Ingredients
1lb smoked salmon
1 bunch fresh dill
4eggs
1 celeriac (1/2 inch thick pieces)
1 tablespoons coconut oil
1 onion minced
1 cup coconut milk

Method
1. Preheat the oven to 375f/ gas mark 5/ 190c or 170c in a fab assisted oven. Coat a baking dish in oil.
2. Fry the onion in a skillet pan with the coconut oil and season with salt.

3. In a mixing bowl, whisk the eggs and coconut milk.
4. Assemble the celeriac slices on the baking dish and top with 1/3 onions and 1/3 dill and 1/3 salmon. Pour ¼ coconut and egg mixture
5. Repeat step 4 layering the ingredients and finish with coconut milk on the top.
6. Cover with foil and bake in the oven for 40 minutes. Remove the foil and cook for a further 10 minutes.

Nutritional content
491 calories, 30g fat, 33g protein, 22g carbohydrates, 4g fibre

HONEY GLAZED COD

Prep time- 5 minutes
Cook time- 15 minutes
Serves 4
Egg free
Nut free

Ingredients
4cod fillets
2 tablespoons minced shallots
1teaspoon coconut oil
¼ cup balsamic vinegar
2tablespoons honey
Salt and pepper

Method
1. Preheat the oven to 425f/ gas mark 7/ 220c or 200c in a fan assisted oven. Coat a baking dish in oil.
2. Add the cod to the dish once both sides have been seasoned with salt and pepper.

3. Whisk together shallots, honey and balsamic vinegar. Pour half the glaze over the cod.
4. *Bake* for 10 minutes and then add the rest of the glaze for a further 5 minute. Serve while hot.

Nutritional content
232 calories, 3g fat, 38g protein, 12g carbohydrates, 0g fibre

Poultry

HONEY GLAZED CHICKEN TARRAGON WITH DIJON DRESSED LETTUCE

Prep time- 10 minutes and 8 hours to marinade
Cook time- 20 minutes
Serves 4

Ingredients
8 boneless chicken thighs
2 head of butter lettuce
2 tablespoons minced tarragon
2 tablespoons minced shallots
1 tablespoon Dijon mustard
2 tablespoons lemon juice
2 tablespoons honey
¼ cup virgin oil
Salt and pepper

Method

1. Whisk shallots, olive oil, lemon juice, honey, mustard and tarragon along with some salt and pepper to make a marinade.
2. Put the chicken in a baking dish and pour over half the marinade. Cover and place in the fridge for at least 8 hours.
3. Preheat the oven to 425f/ gas mark 7/ 220c or 200 in a fan assisted oven
4. Bake for 20 minutes and then shred the chicken into bite sized pieces.
5. Serve the lettuce with the remaining marinade over it and the chicken on top.

Nutritional content

332 calories, 19g fat, 29g protein, 11g carbohydrates, 1g fat

ROSEMARY CHICKEN AND BACON SALAD

Prep time- 10 minutes

Cook time- 15 minutes

Serves 4

Dietary requirements

Egg free

Nut free

Allergen free

Ingredients

1lb chicken breast

4 slices bacon

1 tablespoon rosemary

¼ cup dried cranberries

1 sliced avocado

8 cups mixed greens

2 tablespoons white wine vinegar

1 tablespoon honey

1 teaspoon Dijon mustard

2 tablespoons extra virgin olive oil

Salt and pepper

Method

1. Grill the bacon for 10 minutes and retain the fat in a bowl and set aside. Put the cooked bacon in a dish.
2. Season the chicken with salt and pepper and rosemary. Fry the chicken for 6 minutes on both sides.

3. Take 1 tablespoon of bacon fat and add to a bowl with white wine vinegar, honey, mustard and olive oil and cover with a lid and shake.
4. In a large bowl, toss the salad with the dressing.
5. Serve with chicken on top of salad and sliced avocado, bacon and cranberries.

Nutritional content
354 calories, 11g fat, 30g protein, 17g carbohydrates, 5g fibre

TASTY COB SALAD

As above but add more protein and less carbs. Winner winner tasty cob salad for dinner!!! Add hard boiled eggs to the salad instead of rosemary, honey and cranberries.

Nutritional content
387 calories, 24g fat, 37g protein, 7g carbohydrates, 5g fibre

CREAMY CHICKEN THIGHS IN A MUSHROOM AND PORT SAUCE

Prep time- 5 minutes
Cook time- 15 minutes
Serves 4
Dietary requirements
Egg free
Nut free
Allergen free

Ingredients
8 boneless chicken thighs

1 cup mushrooms

2tablespoons minced shallots

¼ cup port

1/3 cup coconut milk

1 tablespoons virgin oil

salt and pepper

Method
1. Season chicken with salt and pepper. In a skillet fry for 3 minutes on each side and then put on a plate.
2. Fry mushrooms for 5 minutes and then add shallots for and fry for 2 minutes.
3. Add port to the pan and simmer for 3 minutes.
4. Add coconut milk and chicken and cook until chicken is cooked through.

Nutritional content

290 calories, 16 g fat, 28g protein, 3g carbohydrates, 0g fibre

CREAMY CHICKEN THIGHS IN WHITE WINE AND GARLIC MUSHROOM SAUCE

Instead of the shallots use 1 tablespoon minced garlic and 1 tablespoon minced rosemary. Instead of using port use ½ cup white wine.

Nutritional content

390 calories, 16 g fat, 28g protein, 3g carbohydrates, 0g fibre

GARLIC AND HERB CHICKEN

Prep time- 10 minutes

Cook time- 45 minutes

Serve 4

Dietary requirements

Egg free

Nut free

Allergen free

Ingredients

1 full chicken

1 tablespoon minced thyme

1 tablespoon minced rosemary

1 tablespoon minced parsley

2tablespoons extra virgin olive oil

Salt and pepper

Method

1. Preheat the oven to 400f/ gas mark 6/ 200c or 180 in a fan assisted oven.
2. Season the open cavity of chicken with salt and pepper. Place chicken on a baking tray and flatten as much as possible.
3. Run the garlic over the top of the chicken and drizzle with oil.
4. Season the chicken with salt and pepper, rosemary, parsley and thyme. Roast for 45-60 minutes until juices run clear and is cooked through.

Nutritional content

434 calories, 32g fat, 34g protein, 1g carbohydrates, 0g fibre

HARVEST CHICKEN BOWL

Dietary requirements

Egg free

Prep time- 10 minutes
Cook time-none

Ingredients
1 cups shredded chicken
Balsamic Brussel sprouts
Roasted sweet potatoes
2 tablespoons balsamic vinegar
½ tablespoon extra virgin olive oil
½ cup mulled wine cranberry sauce
½ cup maple sliced pecans
8 cups shredded kale
1 tablespoon minced shallots
1 tablespoon maple syrup

Method
1. Whisk the shallots, maple syrup, balsamic vinegar, oil and salt and pepper in bowl. Add the kale and coat.
2. Add the kale and dressing to serving plates to the serving plates and top with the chicken, sprouts, sweet potatoes, cranberries and pecans.

Nutritional content
739 calories, 39g fat, 30g protein, 77g carbohydrates, 16g fibre

CILANTRO GINGER CHICKEN

Dietary requirements
Egg free
Nut free
Allergen free

Prep time- 5 minutes
Cook time- 45 minutes
Serves 4

Ingredients
4chicken legs
8cloves garlic
1 tablespoon chopped cilantro
2 tablespoons lime juice
¼ cup extra virgin olive oil
Salt and pepper

Method
1. In a blender, purée cilantro, ginger, garlic, lime juice, oil and salt and pepper until smooth.
2. Put the chicken in a baking tray and coat in sauce. Put in the fridge for 8 hours to marinade.
3. Preheat the oven to 400f
4. Cook the chicken 5 mins each side in a skillet pan over the hob then bake in the oven for 35 minutes.

Nutritional content
648 calories, 52g fat, 46g protein, 0g carbohydrates, 0g fibre

COMFORTING CHICKEN POT PIE

Prep time- 15 minutes
Cook time- 60 minutes
Serves 6

Ingredients

2lb chicken thighs (1 inch pieces)

1 Sweet Potato (1/2 inch pieces)

1 egg

1 minced onion

4 diced carrots

1 celery sticks minced

1 cup chicken broth

1 tablespoon minced thyme

1 teaspoon minced rosemary

1 tablespoons tapioca starch

1-2 tablespoon iced water

3 tablespoons extra virgin olive oil

2 cups almond flour

2 tablespoon coconut flour

¼ cup palm shortening

Salt and pepper

Method

1. Preheat the oven to 375f/ gas mark 5/ 190c or 170c in a fan assisted oven
2. For the crust:

   In a food processor, pulse almond flour, coconut flour and ½ salt. Add egg, shortening and tablespoon of iced water. Pulse a couple of times to form a dough and leave to side.
3. For the filling:

   On a stove, cook the chicken for 5 minutes on each side. Put on serving plate.
4. Add carrots, onions and celery and cook for 5 minutes and add sweet potatoes and cook for 5 minutes.
5. Stir in the tapioca starch and mix well until dissolved. Then add thyme, rosemary, chicken and chicken broth. Simmer for a minute and remove pan from the heat.
6. Place the filling in the bake tray.
7. Roll the dough out and cover the pie dish. Cut around the edges with a knife to remove excess. Press around the edges of the pie dish to seal then with a knife make a small slit in centre.
8. Bake for 40 minutes

Nutritional content
542 calories, 39g fat, 29g protein, 25g carbohydrates and 8g fibre

MOROCCAN CHICKEN

Dietary requirements
Egg free
Prep time- 5 minutes
Cook time- 45 minutes
Serves 4

Ingredients
1 whole chicken
½ lemon sliced
½ orange sliced
½ chicken broth
1 cup olives
½ cup dried apricots
½ cup roasted almonds
2 tablespoons extra virgin olive oil
1 Tablespoon ginger
1 teaspoon cumin
1 teaspoon cinnamon
Salt and pepper

Method
1. Preheat the oven to 425f/ gas mark 7/ 220c or 200c
2. Put the slices of lemon and orange under the chicken skin and coat skin in oil.
3. In a dish, mix together cinnamon, ginger, cumin salt and pepper and season the chicken with this mixture.

4. Roast chicken for 30 minutes. Baste with the juices and then add olives, apricots, almonds and broth.
5. Roast for 15 minutes.

Nutritional content
415 calories, 23g fat, 35g protein, 16g carbohydrates, 3g fibre

CHICKEN AND WINE REDUCTION

Dietary requirements
Egg free
Nut free
Allergen free

Prep time- 10 minutes
Cook time- 15 minutes
Serves 4

Ingredients
4boneless chicken breasts ½ inch thick
1 Tablespoons extra virgin olive oil
2 zucchini (in chunks)
1 minced clove garlic
½ cup dry red wine
1 teaspoon minced thyme
Salt and pepper

Method
1. Cook chicken in a skillet for 3-4 minutes each side to seal. Set aside.
2. Cook the zucchini for 4 minutes then add garlic for 1 minute. Transfer to bowl with chicken.

3. Heat the wine and thyme to same pan the chicken was in and simmer for 5 minutes.

Nutritional content
367 calories, 13g fat, 54g protein, 5g carbohydrates, 2g fibre

CHICKEN ALFREDO WITH FETTUCCINE

Dietary requirements
Egg free

Prep time- 10 minutes
Cook time- 9 minutes
Serves 4

Ingredients
16 ounces chicken tenders
½ cup cashews
1 full garlic bulb (roasted)
1 teaspoon thyme
Grain free Fettuccine
1 tablespoon extra virgin olive oil
Salt and pepper

Method
1. Cook chicken over he stove for 5 minutes each side.
2. For sauce:
Place the garlic, coconut milk, cashews and thyme in a blender and purée until smooth. Add sauce to the pan and simmer for 2 minutes.
3. Book the pasta in water for 90 seconds then drain. Save ½ cup pasta water.

Nutritional content
421 calories, 21g fat, 33g protein, 25g carbohydrates, 1g fibre

ROASTED CHICKEN AND BACON WITH ORANGE SAUCE

Prep time- 10 minutes
Cook time- 45 minutes
Serves 4

Ingredients
4 slices bacon
4 small chickens
1 Cup fresh orange juice
1 sliced kamquats
1 tablespoon sherry vinegar
Salt and pepper

Method
1. Preheat the oven to 375f/ gas mark 5/ 190c or 170c in a fan assisted oven.
2. Cook the bacon in a skillet pan for 10 minutes and transfer to a dish.keep the fat separate.
3. Season chickens with salt and pepper and coat in bacon fat. Roast for 25 minutes.
4. Whilst cooking, add to the same skillet the orange juice and kumquats and simmer for 10 minutes. Add honey and vinegar and cook until thickens.
5. Briefly remove chicken from oven to pour orange sauce over them then continue to cook for 10-15 minutes. Serve with the bacon.

Nutritional content
667 calories, 41g fat, 57g protein, 18g carbohydrates, 3g fibre

PAD THAI CHICKEN

Prep time- 10 minutes
Cook time- 15 minutes
Serves 4

Ingredients

1lb chicken breast tenders

4 carrots spiralised or strips

4 eggs (whisked)

2 tablespoons coconut oil

1 tablespoon minced garlic

1 tablespoon minced ginger

3 tablespoons fish sauce

¼ cup lime juice

1 tablespoon honey

4 scallions (sliced)

½ cup cilantro

½ cup cashews

Salt and pepper

Method

1. Heat the coconut oil in a skillet and add the egg for two minutes then flip for 30 seconds. Fold into ¼ and slice into thin strips on a chopping board.
2. Fry the chicken for 5 minutes and set aside.
3. Cook the carrots in the skillet for 3 minutes and then add garlic and ginger for another 2 minutes.
4. Whisk the fish sauce, lime juice and honey in a small bowl and pour in the pan. Add scallions for 2-3 minutes.
5. Return the eggs and chicken to the pan and toss gently. To serve, garnish with cilantro and cashews.

Nutritional content
398 calories, 23g fat, 36g protein, 13g carbohydrates, 1g fibre

CHICKEN AND SAUSAGE CASSOULET

Dietary requirements
Egg free
Nut free
Allergen free
Prep time- 10 minutes
Cook time- 60 minutes
Serves 4

Ingredients
4skin on chicken thighs
4ounces pork chunks
2garlic sausage links
1minced onion
2minced carrots
1 minced celery
1 tablespoon minced garlic
2 bay leaves
1 tablespoon thyme
4cups chicken broth
¼ cup dry white wine
Salt and pepper

Method
1. Preheat the oven to 425f/ gas mark 7/ 220c or 200c in a fan assisted oven.

2. Brown the pork for 10 minutes and put on a plate.
3. Dear the chicken for 5 minutes each side and set aside.
4. Cook sausage in the same pan for 4 minutes and set aside.
5. Add carrots, onion, celery, bay leaves, garlic and thyme and salt and pepper to the pan and cook for 5-7 minutes.
6. Being to simmer and add wine and broth, sausage, chicken, pork.
7. Bake for 30 minutes.

Nutritional content
504 calories, 339g fat, 43g protein, 5g carbohydrates, 1g fibre

DUCK WITH CABERNET THYME

Dietary requirements
Egg free
Nut free
Allergen free

Prep time- 5 minutes
Cook time- 22 minutes
Serves 4

Ingredients
4duck breasts
1 shallot sliced
1 thyme sprig
1 cup Cabernet
Salt and pepper

Method
1. Preheat the oven to 350f/ gas mark 4/ 180c or 160c in a fan assisted oven.

2. Season duck in salt and pepper and skillet skin side down for 5 minutes.
3. Add shallot and thyme and roast for 5 minutes.
4. Remove the duck to rest.
5. Pour Cabernet in pan and simmer for 10 minutes. Discard the thyme and shallots.
6. Serve with slices of duck drizzled with the wine jus.

Nutritional content
418 calories, 19g fat, 46g protein, 2g carbohydrates, 0g fibre

CHICKEN THIGHS WITH KABOCHA AND PARSNIPS

Dietary requirements
Egg free
Nut free
Allergen free
Prep time- 10 minutes
Cook time- 50 minutes
Serves 4

Ingredients
1 Kabocha squash (cubed)
1 parsnips in halves
6 carrots in halves
1 red onion wedges
4 bone in chicken thighs
Salt and pepper

Method
1. Preheat the oven to 400f/ gas mark 6/ 200c or 180c in a fan assisted oven.

2. Assemble the squash, parsnips, carrots and onion on a baking tray and drizzle with coconut oil.
3. Sear the chicken for 10 minutes and then flip over for 5 minutes. Add chicken to the veg and roast for another 15 minutes.

Nutritional content
345 calories, 17g fat, 17g protein, 34g carbohydrates, 7g fibre

CHICKEN THIGHS WITH MUSHROOMS AND ASPARAGUS

As above but use 1 pint of mushrooms, asparagus and garlic instead of the squash, parsnips, carrots and onions.

Nutritional content
241 calories, 17g fat, 17g protein, 5g carbohydrates, 2g fibre

Beef pork and lamb

GINGER PORK LETTUCE CUPS

Prep time- 10 minutes
Cook time- 7 minutes
Serves 4

Ingredients
1lb ground pork
1 tablespoon minced ginger
1 tablespoon minced garlic
1 tablespoon toasted sesame oil
2 tablespoons gluten free soy sauce
1 tablespoon lime juice
8 butter lettuce leaves
½ cup cilantro
2sliced green onions
1 carrot
¼ chopped cashews
Salt and pepper

Method
1. Cook pork in a skillet with oil for 5 minutes
2. Add ginger, garlic, and cook for 2 minutes
3. Add soy sauce, lime juice and cook for 1 minute
4. To serve, place pork between each lettuce leaf And top with cilantro, green onions, carrots and chopped cashews

Nutritional content

431 calories, 31g fat, 31g protein, 6g carbohydrates, 1g fibre

SLOW COOKED BEEF AND VEG STEW

Dietary requirements
Egg free
Nut free
Allergen free
Prep time- 10 minutes
Cook time- 8 hours
Serves 4

Ingredients
2lb beef chunks
2 chopped parsnips
1 cup wine
1 cups beef broth
1 cup diced onion
1 tablespoon extra virgin olive oil
1 diced celery
2smashed garlic cloves
1 bay leaf
1 carrots chopped
1 chopped turnip

Method
1. Place all of the ingredients in a slow cooker ensuring the liquid covers the contents. Add some water or more broth to ensure they are covered.
2. Cover with a lid and cook on low setting for 8 hours.

Nutritional content
444 calories, 18g fat, 4g protein, 23g carbohydrates, 6g fibre

CHILLI CON CARNE

Dietary requirements
Egg free
Nut free
Allergen free
Prep time- 10 minutes
Cook time – 1 hour 20 minutes
Serves 4

Ingredients
2lb beef chunks
1 cup diced onions
1 cup diced celery
1 cup diced carrots
1 cup peeled and diced beets
1 cloves garlic smashed
1 tablespoon extra virgin olive oil
1 tablespoon cumin
1 teaspoon coriander
Pinch of cinnamon
1 cup red wine
2cups beef broth
¼ cup minced cilantro
1 avocado sliced
Salt and pepper

Method

1. Fry beef in oil for 10 mins and place in a separate dish
2. Add onions, celery, carrots and beetroots to the pan and cook for 5 mins. Add garlic and cook for 2 more minutes
3. Add cumin, coriander and cinnamon and cook for 1 minute
4. Add red wine and simmer for 2 minutes
5. Cook for one hour and garnish with cilantro and avocado

Nutritional content
470 calories, 25g fat, 46g protein, 16g carbohydrates, 6g fibre

FLANK STEAK BURRITO BOWL

Dietary requirements
Egg free
Nut free
Allergen free
Prep time- 5 minutes
Cook time- 10 minutes
Serves 4

Ingredients
1 flank steak
4 cups romaine lettuce
1 teaspoon minced garlic
1 teaspoon minced cumin
1 teaspoon minced oregano
1 teaspoon minced pepper
2 tablespoons lime juice
2 tablespoons extra virgin olive oil
¼ teaspoon salt
Roasted sweet potatoes

½ cup guacamole

¼ cup minced red onion

¼ cup minced cilantro

Method
1. In a zip bag, add garlic, cumin, oregano, lime juice, salt and pepper, olive oil and the steak and marinade in fridge for 8-12 hours
2. Grill steak for 5 minutes on each side and set aside to rest
3. Divide lettuce between serving bowls and top with sweet potatoes
4. Finish with guacamole, red onion, and cilantro

Nutritional content
477 calories, 30g fat, 27g protein, 29g carbohydrates, 7g fibre

PEPPERCORN BEEF AND BROCCOLI

Dietary requirements
Egg free
Nut free
Allergen free
Prep time- 5 minutes
Cook time- 18 minutes

Ingredients
1 boneless rib eye steak
1 broccoli
1 tablespoon coconut oil
1 tablespoon sesame oil
1 tablespoon minced garlic
1 teaspoon minced ginger
¼ cup soy sauce

1 tablespoons lime juice

2sliced scallions

Salt and pepper

Method
1. Season steak with salt and pepper and fry for 5 minutes each side
2. Sauté broccoli for 5 minutes, add garlic and ginger and cook for 1 minute. Add soy sauce and lime juice and cook for 1 minute
3. Slice the steak and return to the pan to toss before serving.

Nutritional content

314 calories, 25g fat, 19g protein, 4g carbohydrates, 1g fibre

SAGE ROASTED PORK WITH APRICOT SAUCE

Dietary requirements

Egg free

Nut free

Allergen free

Prep time- 5 minutes

Cook time- 25 minutes

Serves 4

Ingredients

1 ¼ lb pork tenderloins

2tablespoons minced sage

1 cloves garlic

1 minced shallot

Cup of Riesling

½ cup chicken broth

½ cup chopped apricots

1 tablespoons extra virgin olive oil

Method
1. Grind the garlic, salt and pepper and sage to form a paste and then mix in the olive oil
2. Rub the mixture over the pork tenderloins
3. Roast for 25 minutes
4. Cook shallots, apricots, chicken broth and resiling on the hob until apricots are tender.
5. Blend until a smooth sauce
6. Let the pork rest for 10 minutes and then slice into medallions. Serve with the apricot jus over the top of the pork.

Nutritional content
390 calories, 19g fat, 43g protein, 11g carbohydrates, 1g fibre

ROSEMARY PORK WITH PLUM WINE SAUCE

Use rosemary instead of sage. Instead of Riesling use dried plums and full bodied red wine.

Nutritional content
390 calories, 19g fat, 43g protein, 11g carbohydrates, 1g fibre

GINGER AND COCONUT PORK SKEWERS

Prep time 5 minutes
Cook time- 10 minutes
Serves 4

Ingredients

1 ¼ lb pork tenderloins cut into pieces

1 tablespoon minced ginger

½ cup coconut milk

2 tablespoons lime juice

1 tablespoon brown sugar

1teaspoon ground turmeric

1teaspoon ground coriander

½ teaspoon ground cumin

Salt and pepper

Method

1. Whisk coconut milk, lime juice, ginger, brown sugar m, turmeric, coriander, cumin and salt and pepper and coat the pork
2. Marinade in the fridge for 8 hours
3. Place the pork on skewers and grill for 5 minutes each side

Nutritional content

352 calories, 17g fat, 42g protein, 6g carbohydrates, 0g fibre

CITRUS PORK TENDERLOINS

Prep time- 10 minutes

Cook time- 25 minutes

Serves 4

Ingredients

1 ¼ lbs pork tenderloins

1 minced cloves garlic

¼ cup freshly squeezed orange juice

3 tablespoons freshly squeezed lime juice

1 tablespoon minced oregano

1 teaspoon ground cumin

½ cup minced cilantro

¼ cup extra virgin olive oil

Salt and pepper

Method
1. In a zip bag add the pork, salt and pepper, garlic, oil, cilantro, orange and lime juice, oregano and cumin. Marinade for 8 hours.
2. Preheat the oven to 325f/ gas mark 3/ 170c or 150c in fan assisted oven
3. Seal the meat in a skillet pan and then cook in oven for 15 minutes allow to rest for 10 minutes

Nutritional content

416 calories, 25g fat, 42g protein, 2g carbohydrates, <1g fibre

PEPPERCORN CRUSTED PORK CHOPS

Prep time- 5 minutes

Cook time- 25 minutes

Serves 4

Ingredients

4 pork chops

4 tablespoons extra virgin olive oil

2tablespoons coarsely ground peppercorns

1 heads endive

1 tea minced garlic

1 lemon zest and Juice

½ cup chicken broth

Salt

Method

1. Season pork with peppercorns and salt. Dear on each side for 6-8 minutes until cooked throughout. Put separately.
2. Cook the endives in the pan for 5 minutes until browned
3. Add garlic, lemon zest and juice and chicken broth. Cover the lid and cook for 5 minutes and serve with the pork chops.

Nutritional content
360 calories, 24g fat, 35g protein, 10g carbohydrates, 10g fibre

PORK CHOPS AND MUSHROOMS

Dietary requirements
Egg free
Nut free
Allergen free
Prep time- 5 minutes
Cook time- 22 minutes
Serves 4

Ingredients
4boneless pork chops
2Tablespoons extra virgin olive oil
Minced shallot
2 minced cloves garlic
1 teaspoon minced thyme
½ teaspoon minced rosemary
¼ Marsala

Method

1. Season the pork with salt and pepper and zest for 5 minutes each side and transfer to a chopping board
2. Fry mushrooms for 7 minutes
3. Add shallots, thyme, garlic and rosemary and cook 3 minutes
4. Add Marsala until evaporated for approx 2 minutes
5. To serve top pork chops with mushrooms

Nutritional content
333 calories, 16g fat, 47g protein, 4g carbohydrates, <1g fibre

COSTA RICAN RIB EYE STEAK IN COFFEE GLAZE

Dietary requirements
Egg free
Nut free
Allergen free
Prep time- 10 minutes
Cook time- 40 minutes
Serves 4

Ingredients
1lb boneless ribeye steak
1 cup strong coffee
½ cup of dark rum
1 teaspoon peppercorns
1 teaspoon coriander seeds
1 shallot
¼ cup red wine vinegar
¼ cup brown sugar

Method

1. In the saucepan, simmer the coffee, rum, peppercorns, coriander, shallot, red wine vinegar and sugar for 20 minutes. Take out the shallots by straining and coat the glaze on the steak.
2. Grill steak for 10 minutes and then top with more glaze. Cook for another 10 minutes

Nutritional content
439 calories, 34g fat, 34g protein, 12g carbohydrates, 0g fibre

BEEF RIB RAGU FETTUCCINE

Prep time- 10 minutes
Cook time- 2 hours
Serves 4

Ingredients
1lb beef short ribs
1 celery storks
2 diced carrots
1 diced red onion
1 teaspoon minced thyme
1 teaspoon minced rosemary
1 cup red wine
2tablespoons gluten free soy sauce
Grain free Fettuccine
Salt and pepper

Method
1. Season ribs with salt and pepper and sear for 10 minutes
2. Flip ribs add celery, carrots, onion, thyme, and sauté for 5 minutes
3. Pour in red wine and soy sauce and bake for 2 hours

4. Shred the meat and return to the pan
5. Cook pasta in boiling water for 90 seconds. Serve the beef ragu over the pasta

Nutritional content
692 calories, 40g fat, 26g protein, 32g carbohydrates, 5g fibre

BEEF BOURGUIGNON

Prep time- 10 minutes
Cook time- 2 hours
Serve 4

Ingredients
2lbs beef chunks

1 cups mushrooms

2 cups blanched pearl onions

1 tablespoon extra virgin olive oil

4 carrots diced

1 sprig rosemary

Sprig thyme

1 cups dry red wine

2 cups beef broth

1 teaspoon sugar

Salt and pepper

Method
1. Brown meat for 10 minutes leave to rest
2. Fry mushrooms for 2 minutes and then add onions, carrots, rosemary, thyme, red wine, beef broth. Cook for 1 hour.
3. Remove cover, cook for another 65 minutes

Nutritional content
513 calories, 26g fat, 55g protein, 3g carbohydrates, 3g fibre

SOUP OF TUSCANY

Dietary requirements
Egg free
Nut free
Allergen free

Prep time- 10 minutes
Cook time- 40 minutes

Ingredients
1lb ground pork
1 tablespoons minced garlic
Minced onion
2S sweet Potatoes cubed
4 cups chicken broth
Cup of coconut milk
2 cups shredded kale
Tablespoon extra virgin olive oil
Teaspoon fennel crushed
Salt and pepper

Method
1. Cook the pork and fennel in a skillet pan for 10 minutes. transfer to dish
2. Add garlic and onion and continue to cook for 5 minutes
3. Add the sweet potatoes, chicken broth, coconut milk and pork and simmer for 20 minutes
4. Add kale for last 5 minutes

ARGENTINE GRILLED LAMB CHOPS

Dietary requirements
Egg free
Nut free
Allergen free
Prep time- 5 minutes
Cook time- 20 minutes
Serves 4

Ingredients
4 lamb chops
4 cloves chopped garlic
½ red onion chopped
¼ cup chopped parsley
¼ cup chopped mint
2 tablespoons red wine vinegar
¼ cup extra virgin olive oil
Salt and pepper

Method
1. In a blender, purée the garlic, onion, parsley, mint, red wine, oil and salt and pepper until smooth. Paste the lamb chops in the mixture and marinade for 30 mins to 8 hours in the fridge.
2. Grill the chops 10 minutes on each side

Nutritional content
353 calories, 23g fat, 35g protein, 2g carbohydrates, 1g fibre

MEAT LOAF

Prep time- 15 minutes
Cook time- 1 hour 10 minutes

Ingredients
4slices of bacon
1lb ground beef
1lb ground pork
A whisked egg
Cup minced onion
½ cup minced celery
½ cup minced carrots
Teaspoon minced garlic
Teaspoon minced rosemary
¼ cup minced parsley
½ cup almond flour
Tablespoon extra virgin olive oil
Salt and pepper

Method
1. Preheat the oven to 350f/ gas mark 4/ 180c or 160c in a fan assisted oven
2. Cook the onion, carrots, celery, garlic, rosemary and parsley for 10 minutes.
3. In a bowl, mix in the flour, egg and salt and pepper to make a paste and mix in the vegetables and meat.
4. Transfer to a meat loaf tin and top with bacon slices.
5. Bake for 1 hour

Nutritional content
434 calories, 34g fat, 28g protein, 4g carbohydrates, 2g fibre

MEATBALL MARINARA

Prepare the meatloaf ingredients as above but leave out the bacon. Make 16 balls out of the mixture and sear until browned. Pour tomato free Mariana sauce and bake for 30 minutes

Nutritional content
462 calories, 40g fat, 28g protein, 15g carbohydrates, 4g fibre

ROASTED RIB

Prep time- 10 minutes
Cook time- 1 hour 30 minutes

Ingredients
Rib roast
Minced garlic (2 tablespoons)
Minced garlic (3 tablespoons)
Tablespoon minced rosemary
Extra virgin olive oil (3 tablespoons)
Salt and pepper

Method
1. Make a thick paste using the garlic, rosemary, oil salt and pepper and coat the meat. Marinade in fridge for 8 hours.
2. Preheat the oven to 450f/ gas mark 8/ 230c or 210 in a fan assisted oven

3. Roast for 30 minutes and then reduce the heat to 325f and roast for another hour.

Nutritional content
413 calories, 25g fat, 43g protein, 0g carbohydrates, 0g fibre

MEDITERRANEAN STYLE LAMB KEBABS

Prep time- 5 minutes
Cook time- 15 minutes
Serves 4

Ingredients
1lb boneless lamb chops cut into chunks
Chopped red onion
Tablespoon extra virgin olive oil
Teaspoon ground cumin
Teaspoon ground sumac
¼ cup tahini
Tablespoon tahin
Tablespoon minced garlic
2 tablespoons red wine vinegar
Sliced cucumber
A cup of olives
Salt and pepper

Method
1. Preheat the oven to 400f/ gas mark 6/ 200c or 180c in a fan assisted oven
2. Thread the meat and onion into the skewers to make the kebabs
3. Coat in oil and season with cumin, sumac and salt and pepper
4. Roast for 15 minutes

5. Whilst cooking, whisk garlic, lemon juice, tahini and red wine vinegar and drizzle over the cucumber and onion to serve with the cooked kebabs

Nutritional content
359 calories, 25g fat, 27g protein, 9g carbohydrates, 2g fibre

Desserts

NO BAKE COCONUT BARS

Prep time- 10 minutes
Cook time- 0 minutes
Serves 12

Ingredients
1 tablespoons unsweetened coco powder
11/4 shredded coconut flakes
2 tablespoons cacao nibs
11/4 cups peacan nuts
¼ salt
2 dates pitted and chopped
½ cup coconut oil
Vanilla bean
3 tablespoons maple syrup

Method:
1. Pulse cocoa powder, 1 cup pecans and salt in a food processor until coarse. Add dates and pulse to make a mixture.
2. Press the mixture into the bottom of a tray
3. In a bowl, mix coconut oil, vanilla and maple syrup. Stir in 1 cup of coconut flakes. Spoon this mixture over the top of the other mix in the baking tray. Serve with peacans, coco flakes and cacao nibs sprinkled on top.
4. Cut into 12 portions and top with parchment paper
5. Leave to cool in a fridge for at least 15 minutes

Nutritional content
240 calories, 24h fat, 2g protein, 9g carbohydrates, 3g fibre

VANILLA CHOCOLATE TRUFFLES

Dietary requirements
Egg free
Nut free
Allergen free
Vegan

Prep time- 15 minutes
Cook time- 5 minutes
Serves 24

Ingredients
7 ounces dark chocolate chopped
11/2 tablespoons vanilla extract
¼ cup cocoa powder
½ cup coconut milk
Salt

Method
1. In a small pan, cook the coconut milk and salt on a low heat on a hob.
2. Add chocolate to pan and heat until almost melted. Stir occasionally
3. Add vanilla extract and then place in the fridge for 1 hour until hard
4. Put cocoa powder in bowl and then make 24 balls out of the mixture
5. Roll the balls in the cocoa powder and serve at room temperature

Nutritional content
158 calories, 14g fat, 7g protein, 8g carbohydrates, 5g fibre

THIN MINTS

Dietary requirements
Egg free
Vegan
Prep time- 10 minutes
Cook time- 0
Serves 24

Ingredients
½ cup magic chocolate sauce
Tablespoon cacao nibs
¼ teaspoon peppermint oil
1 tablespoon cocoa powder
egg walnut
Cup of dates

Method
1. Mix dates and walnuts in the food processor until smooth. Add cocoa powder and salt and pulse. Add a dash of peppermint oil and pulse some more. Add cacao nibs and pulse again.
2. Line a bake tray with parchment paper and make flat shapes out of the mixture
3. Place in freezer for 20 minutes
4. Dunk the mints in chocolate sauce and freeze for 5 minutes

Nutritional content
100 calories, 8g fat, 1g protein, 8g carbohydrates, 2g fibre

FROZEN CHOCOLATE BANANAS

Dietary requirements

Egg free

Nut free

Allergen free

Prep time- 5 minutes

Cook- 0

Serves 12

Ingredients

1   sliced bananas

½ cup magic chocolate sauce

Method

1. Freeze the banana slices for 50 minutes
2. Dip banana in chocolate and freeze for 10 minutes. Store in freezer

Nutritional content

122 calories, 10g fat, 1g protein, 11g carbohydrates, 2g fibre

MAGIC CHOCOLATE SAUCE

Makes ½ cup

Ingredients

Tablespoon maple syrup

½ cup coconut oil

¼ cup cocoa powder

Salt

Method

1. Whisk all ingredients together and store in fridge.

Nutritional content

130 calories, 14g fat, 1g protein, 3g carbohydrates, 1g fibre

CHOCOLATE ALMOND BUTTER CUPS

Dietary requirements
Egg free
Vegan
Prep time- 10 minutes
Cook- 10 minutes

Ingredients
Cup of almond butter
¼ cup maple syrup
½ cup coconut oil
½ cup cocoa powder

Method
1. In a blender pulse coconut oil, ½ cup almond butter and maple syrup.
2. Add in coco powder, salt and blend
3. With half the mixture pour in the muffin trays and place in the fridge for 10 minutes.
4. Scoop the rest of the almond butter into the chocolate cups. Pour the rest of the chocolate mix on top.
5. Place in the fridge for at least 30 minutes

Nutritional content
235 calories, 21g fat, 4g protein, 11g carbohydrates, 3g fibre

MAPLE ICE CREAM

Dietary requirements
Egg free
Vegan
Serves 7

Ingredients
Cup almond milk
Can of coconut milk
¼ cup tahini
½ cup maple syrup
Tablespoon white miso
Tablespoon vanilla extract

Method
1. Mix all the ingredients in a blender and pour into an ice cream maker.
2. Transfer ice cream to a container and freeze until firm.

Nutritional content
194 calories, 13g fat, 3g protein, 17g carbohydrates, 1g fibre

CHOCOLATE ICE CREAM

Dietary requirements
Egg free
Nut free
Allergen free
Vegan

Serves 8

Ingredients

4 ounces dairy free dark chocolate

2 tablespoons coconut palm sugar

Can coconut milk

Cup almond milk

Tablespoon brewed coffee

Method

    1.heat all the ingredients (except the chocolate). When the sugar is dissolved add the   chocolate until melted.

    2   Cover with parchment paper and place in the fridge for 20 minutes

    3   Pour in the ice cream maker and churn for 20 minutes and then freeze until firm.

Nutritional content

143 calories, 12g fat, 2g protein, 10g carbohydrates, 2g fibre

HAZELNUT AND MAPLE CHOCOLATE TORTE

Dietary requirements

Egg free

Vegan

Serves 12

Ingredients

6 ounces cacao chocolate

2 cups ground hazelnuts

Tablespoon palm sugar

Teaspoon salt

1 tablespoons bourbon

2 tablespoons shortening

¾ coco cream

½ cup maple syrup

3 teaspoons vanilla extract

Method
1. Preheat the oven to 350f/ gas mark 4/ 180c or 160c in a fan assisted oven
2. In a bowl, mix hazelnuts, sugar and salt. Pour in the shortening and a teaspoon of vanilla extract
3. Press the mix into the bottom of a baking tray
4. To make the filling:

    ½ cup coco cream, syrup, vanilla extract, salt and bourbon. Simmer.

    Stir in the chocolate no then rest for 5 minutes.

    Stir in ¼ cup coconut cream
5. Place in the fridge for at least 2-3 hours

Nutritional content
273 calories, 23g fat, 5g protein, 17g carbohydrates,4g fibre

SPICE PEAR CRISPS

Dietary requirements
Egg free
Vegan
Serves 8

Ingredients
8 diced pears
¼ cup brown sugar
Cup of almond flour
¼ cup tapioca starch
Tablespoon and one teaspoon of 5 spice powder

Method
1. Preheat the oven to 350f/ gas mark 4/ 180c or 160c in a fan assisted oven

2. Coat a baking tray in shortening
3. Place the pears in the baking tray and season with tapioca starch and five spice
4. Mix two tablespoons tapioca starch m, tablespoon five spice, almond flour, salt and sugar in a bowl. Add palm shortening
5. Sprinkle topping over the pears and bake 25 minutes

Nutritional content
245 calories, 14g fat, 4g protein, 33g carbohydrates, 6g fibre

BLACK AND BLUEBERRY CRISPS

Replace the pears with 3 cups of blackberries and 3 cups blueberries don't use the five spice and add teaspoon grated lemon zest

Nutritional content
214 calories, 14g fat, 4g protein, 25g carbohydrates, 5g fibre

PEACH AND VANILLA CRUMBLE

Swap the pears for peaches and don't use 5 spice. Add ¼ teaspoon nutmeg and 1 tablespoon vanilla extract

Nutritional content
207 calories, 14g fat, 4g protein, 23g carbohydrates, 4g fibre

PEACH AND MOUSSE

Preheat the oven to 400f/ gas mark 6/ 200c or 180c fan assisted oven

Place 2 tablespoons mousse into the centre of each peach and then sprinkle with cinnamon

Bake for 20 minutes

Nutritional content
190 calories, 13g fat, 1g protein, 11g carbohydrates, 2g fibre

Made in the USA
Lexington, KY
13 July 2018